T0308990

U V W X Y Z A B C
D E F G I J K L M
N O P Q R S T U V W
X Y Z A B C D F G
H I J K L M N O P
R S T V W X Y Z
B C E F G H I J K
L M N O P Q S T U
V W X Y Z B C D E
F H I J K L M N O
P Q R S T U V W X Y
Z A B C D F G H I
J K L M O P Q R S
T U V W X Y Z A B C
D F G H I J K L M
N O P Q R S T U V ●

Larry Price • Roof Books

Copyright © 2008 Larry Price

ISBN-10: 1-931824-31-2
ISBN-13: 978-1-931824-31-6

Library of Congress Catalog Card No.: 2008934769

NYSCA

This book was made possible,
in part, with public funds from
the New York State Council
on the Arts, a state agency.

Roof Books are distributed by:
Small Press Distribution
1341 Seventh Street
Berkeley, CA 94710-1403
Phone orders: 800-869-7553
spdbooks.org

Roof Books are published by
Segue Foundation
300 Bowery
New York, NY 10012
seguefoundation.com

The Quadragene

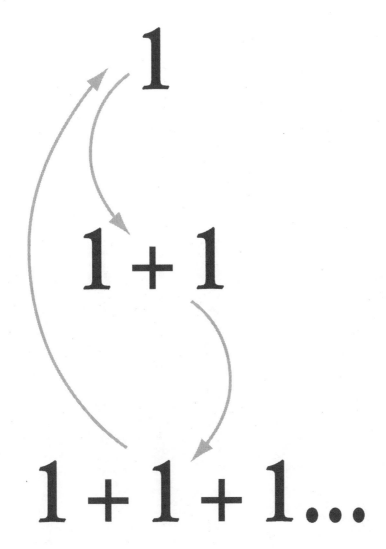

The One who parses and the one who doesn't are not the same. The other's the same, but not both. Both are one, but not the same. The One who's both and the One who isn't are the same. One is both but not the other and so not the same. The empty set of the halves of its Being – the first, the last, the next. The set of the same and not-the-same and the empty set of all that is within all that isn't are one and the same. One is not the same. The one that is is one half of the empty set of the next half of the one who isn't. Neither is the last, and both are neither. Neither the One nor the one which is both is everything. Everything that is is in a set of the empty sets of one, the same, the one-and-the-same, and the one which is neither. I am neither, and neither is the empty set of everything I am. Am I neither the first half? nor the last? I forget, not being both and being the same. Being the same is not a half, and none has enough halves for either. Either makes the whole be dead, the mind in parts $(1 + 1' \ldots ,$ etc.$)$. They run on, more something than mad, more mad than something, while we parts (parts are means without ends) can't stop either. We become the empty set of everything that is. And then something else. Everything that is is something. And then something else. And everything I am is different than something else. The same one who is and the same one in the empty set of the one who is are neither. As we've seen, I am neither, and neither is something else. Something else is the Other, both the one that is and the one that will-have-been when the one that is is everything. Only the one-which-is-not is, and the one which is is not. Both are neither, which is why we are, that is, the set of the one that will-have-been when the one that is is not.

●

Present speech is past speech in a
transferential crisis. An accident in which
art eats art between the worm and the
difference art makes. Art never works
so well as when it speaks in the code
with which it becomes blank again.
Not a void. The short straw in a copular
suspension, where any signifier is rooted
in the bonds that, like wagons, circle in
every self-cancelling direction. There's no
tautology like business, and work itself is
a limit (like discourse or nothing at all).
By discourse, we mean a self-inflected
species willing to leave its own internal
aims. Aimlessly (or inflectively), it follows
the last term toward the next. An alphabet
between which the apprentice riddles to
the sun.

●

A Slipknot in the Memic News

Doubt is the equity in economies of
obedience. It's a simple story: using a
broom to solve the rebus: word, no word,
something, nothing, etc. The Market (or
scissive world) rises when real wages fall.
Everything's been celebrified. Parts within
parts. For which the Revelator is in the
code, and the code is in the skull. Where
we put the right brain in. We take the left
brain out. Then we cut the pages up and
swallow all the doubt.

●

Practicing
My New Brain

There is an oblate black bag we bear
witness to, a time limit on each stingy
sentence. Nothing comes of its interior.
And nothing is what we ask, the certainty
of a phantasm or any disinterested beast.
I.e., words have their meanings. We
have ours. Meanings don't lie. People
do. Having lied, we sleep. The System
never sleeps. In a system, everyone says
that everyone says something. Everyone
who, in the parable of human radius,
shows meaning as all there is. It certainly
is. The bad truth in which our terms
equal the parsimony between us. In the
margin, our parsimony will be redeemed,
if, by redemption, we mean snarling
incessance. Which, as anyone knows, is
a binary condition, i.e., symmetrical and

commutative. Function compulsively
fills every term. It puts the ends in the
blanks, the blanks in us, and leaves them
there. A signifying mandate. If I stay in
Paris, the coin will come up heads. Or in
a sea (a waterfall) to take up arms against.
As for those who can't oppose physical
abstraction, as in eating (being so) or
using what isn't on what is (will be or will
have been) the differences between them
(the halves, and so on), the world turns,
etc. Like an American poet saying: I hate
money. Money is funny, etc. In all the
reasons other than the one that is.

●

Learning to Love
the Dial, the Music
Fiercely Trained

From the brain wall to the other brain
wall, there's a little bit of thorn in every
contingency. For example:

> this old man
> he played one

and came rolling home through the briars
& brambles. The briars that didn't exist
and the brambles that do define the
margin in which the name is an irritant,
a somersault out the office door. Happy
Nothing Day. The American situation
is an agonist's black bag for serving the
lack and watching the Big Board put us to
sleep. There's no shelf life left for outrage.
Round & round the specular jug, flies
parse an inverted weasel. Money doesn't

exist. It's another black bag collecting
salt between halves of a bicameral brain
in which ambient language is only the
ambient name for ambient exuberance,
the small society in a grand lack of terms:
was and/or is and is-not. Lack too is a
brain.

●

In a Caveman, Singing

By the hair on my chinny-chin-chin and
a faceless truth, the present is le Vide
for the future. Things aren't what they
used to be. What things used to be isn't
either . . . whether in the long arm of
contingency or in the longer arm of
inexistence. Contingency is not a law. It's
a headline from the Big Board and the
bigger board of existence, the meadow
where the accountancy of the Big Board
reaches no more accord than the empty
time it empties. In which the past is
past and the Return to a Meadow leaves
behind only documents and tire tracks. No
matter how violent the margin becomes,
such entropy gives rise to nothing. It's
not the fact that the desert has no one in
it, but that the partition, the wall of its
defining stress (its property) is the great

bonfire among us. It functions as a precise
musical score: nothing[1] in that chair,
nothing[2] in me. Any chair is empty until
the wall(s) of our mimetic crisis fill it with
androgynous proof that all that glitters
is gold. Each new proof, reversible and
inversible, shines as an old riddle shines:
not from being one, but because it isn't.
The sentence begins, and it is a sentence,
an equation between the void and the
vexed human. In its absence & throng,
which, to the extent it is a throng, exudes
& dismembers me in compulsory terms
(this is this & that is that), the ownership
my faceless text would be: in power
and cunning, in Reason and absence, in
nothing and not, its iteration to throng as
number is to rhythm, sunshine for le Vide.

●

Five
Inversion
Functions

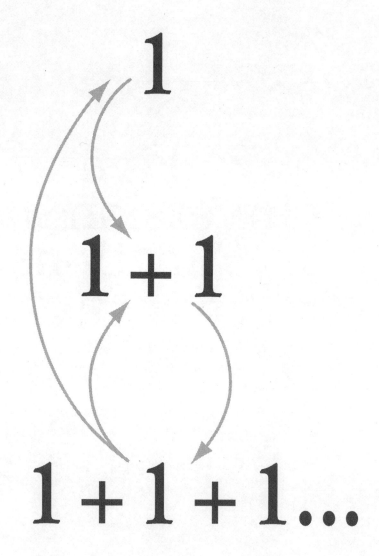

Inversion Function #1:
Specular Backdraft

In this state (which is not a state but a
corporate tumescence), each convenes in
the company of the opposites it keeps.

Nothing could be simpler. Turn the spotlight
on and follow the money. The invisible
tooth in all our lives. Toothless, we see it,
the invisible brawl at our expense.

Your antecedents will thank you. We
won't. We are. It was. And still is, the
wheelbarrow, the inert plums, all the antics
of the specular real. A poetic labor of
nothing binding nothing. Doubly contingent.
The margin in which truth becomes true.

●

Inversion Function

#2: Certain of excess in the uncertain ends of Reason, we mean to be singular in our inverse body of terms

The head is a simple machine, according
to an engine (which is Zeno's) making of
absence time. A complex in one constant
dimension impossible to stop other than
to rage or blindly elect one otherwise
abstract slab of power over another. Only
the name is more abstract, an equation
costing that person that life. Across
its carapace (its self-equation) the first
sentence one might pour onto any dream
or cryptic field (sans number or eye) the
blood-filled margin sings.

●

Inversion Function #3:
Barn Burners

Truth is the ecstasy of dominance and an
empty set of terms. Anything can learn
to write. In fact, here, at Factory Lane
No. Whatever, art was born on the crude,
specular border between thinking and
truth. It's the freedom we spend to keep
the subject equidistant from its articulated
halves. A means to mean. Operands will
be operands. First they mean what they
mean. Then what we mean. And then
they don't. Apertures without recourse. If
we succeed, it isn't necessity, but a wager
inserted into itself. We have nothing to
write that isn't written.

●

Inversion Function #4:
Apocalypse by the zip code

Here, in Fat Land, truth follows truth
into appetite. Appetite, when blind,
is its own truth. Starve the beast and
feed the inversion. What a difference to
inversion each appetitive beast makes. In
inversion, things lived a long time ago.
Now they don't. Our doubles do (and did).
The only useful art is an inversive one,
applying thought as a complaint. Another
semiotic orphan from the interior. This
is its disease, its present. A red-eyed bat
returning in the subjunctive dawn.

●

Inversion Function #5:
What to do with monsters
once the cataclysm stops

How many alpha males does one herd
need? In the market (or fictive world),
every X is incumbent upon us. We solve
them by elimination: one excludes one
+ another one. Thus, to be in is to be
subtensive. To be out, doubly so. Because
being out, we'll never be in, and in,
hysterical about what we start with,
where the mind lingers before breaking
to pieces again, like the word we followed
to this one, there being no X to verify. For
example, take anything. Call it Anything.
Change your mind. Call it: Anything Else.
Things are their own nihilisms. They don't
need me to invert anything. What's good
about nothing is the inversion it already
is. In any case, things don't give pleasure.
People do.

●

In the
Carceral
Storm

I, too, live in a Bunker: the nascent one of Being or the mechanical one of being-not.

For one new symptom, I would sell everything or split into halves.

No one needs more art, just as more & more cash makes cash irrelevant. There's no such thing as more or less truth. Truth empties (absolutely!) the black bags of our existence.

Art promises its beautiful, impotent opposite. The problem is that something and nothing have nothing to add. (Efficacy is not magic.)

So here goes nothing. It happens this way. Then it happens that way, the limit to its limit. An art for its sake and not for ours.

●

We're occludingly reprised creatures in
an auto-consumptive impulse to serve an
impulse on the fat side of the door.

A swarm within fixed eyes making life
particular and riddled with parts. Pick one,
pick any one. As weird as the equal sign (or
consensual void) between dreams.

Which is a terrible thing. We're terrible.
Which isn't so bad.

It being our lunatic incursion into chance,
where what we mean to say buries us in our
own terms: I am. I was. I will have been.

●

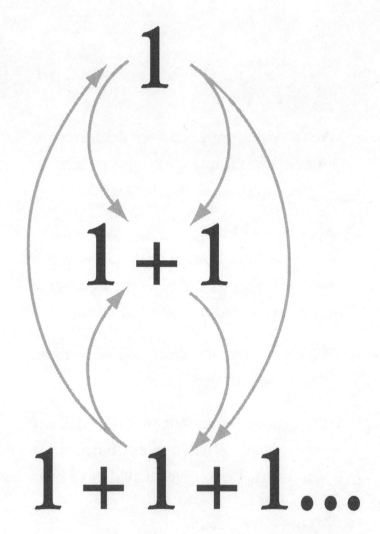

(They say:) either it is, or it isn't. A
certainty "I" contribute to and so prove
even ghosts (or erasures) come back
to life. Species too is a logic, by which
elements (the bones, intrigues and history)
incline the mind to limits. Function buries
everything in limits, the perpetual startup
mode for existence. Its indefatigable
desperation belongs to everyone. It's the
sheer crossed logic of our double game:
loot & be looted. The paroxysm of our
bottomless industrial lease. We're all alike.
It's said (someone says).

●

Saving the skin for last

In the seminal certainty of Being, the old
Dasein isn't what it used to be. The terms
surround us. Wave the Particular good-bye.
A Thing is itself plus the whole it isn't. And
impossibility is to ground as the particular is
to speech. Another half on the fictional route
through omnivorous recall. The form of the
opposite is the same. The same is what we
call artifice in duplicate. That's real. This is
not. This is the same and the opposite. An
opposite is a machine external to the means
by which the same and its same address one
another. A variant of money, the augmented
motion of one's intervalic punition. Address
unknown. So tell me a story. Sell me this for
that. We can deceive the camera with a face,
but not the void behind it. If we go up the
wall, the wall goes with us. If I repeat my

meaning, my meaning wins. Nothing is free. Where shakeable certainty becomes a skin we draw into the obligation to be. To be shaken if the certainty sticks in the undulant reason of Art.

●

We solve X
for half,
solving nothing

Things are more like they are than they
ever were. One world for art and one for
nothing else. We know very well what
we're doing in these soft heads for which
the dogs of our senses run in two's. First,
there's a Figure. And then there's not.
Nothing is itself except le Vide switching
bodies. A transferential term telling its
story in retrospect in the terms of ours.
It takes everything I have – for gossip,
for panic, for pieces of the inverted real.
Everyone has one and maybe is one. And
everyone is somewhere – in the margin
between there and somewhere else,
immune to nothing, with something to
lose. I am one. It is in me something, to
which I add only a term: my term and its

term signifying an algorithm to say what
we say as an unlocatable system for what
the system will have been.

●

What I see
in the
current work

I dreamt Adorno was going to rip my face
off. This is the beginning of a gesture, a
mortality bloom or affluent disease.

Barriers stand for crowd logic and
weekend ganglia. Where staying sane
is a public utility inbreeding activates.
It remains as irreducible as poetry is, a
technology between two others:
one that was and one that will be.

Let poetry equal a dog's tooth. Let a
swarm equal the dog. Poetry is more
useful than a dog without its tooth.

•

As the straw neuter which in the idiosyncrasy of reason does endure its raw existence, meaning is inert until bundled, one single bat in the debt-riddled hum of the spectral world.

Put a name on it. Call it Riddle. Or tell me a story and make me random. A vice on my wish list, whose fact blossoms in my scissive index finger running down its list of things to be or not to be. Where one reason for Reason is reason not to.

•

Or as the new version of an old version, let
my brain strip code of its solipsism, whose
truth, having always to have seized what
we were about to write, leaves us bored.
In the cunning of Art, each term signifies
A or not-A, a drum, which, if we are to be
superfluous, lolling through history with
the feedbag on, must still blaze its ordinal
path, the symptoms it fills with, in transit,
making it readable. Mind is an iteration
of that. No more a void than the numbers
that spoon the brawl into isolated bags.
There's no elemental deep end. The mind's
enclitic soup is a truth for which the price
is uselessness. Before being useful, it isn't.
We owe it to reason to use everything in our
manifest means to mean.

●

The ding-an-sich takes a number

Particulars are monstrous. Monsters
aren't. Monsters serve the uncertain ends
of exchange: one for another one, etc.
Phonemes of an uninterruptible existence
saying what it says. What it means is what
constrains us. What we mean is a slow
drawl of concision blooming in le Vide.
Everything is nothing before it becomes
something else. Everything and nothing,
plus the circle of its parts, who, in one
frame, declare that they can no more
believe in the local and particular than live
without them. In spite of everything, to
be human is an outburst. "I" see "them."
"They" can't see. "We" see us in the
fricative thick of things, where neither
I nor the vessel of my inversions can
contain them.

●

History is
not a placard
for applause

All the world's a Market. We turn surplus
signification into truth (over time). Our
thesis is that that thesis is obscene. In
it, language has become market therapy.
The bell rings, and a figure says, I Smell
Money. A figure is nothing in itself but the
oblate logic of its attachments. A burial of
romance in the ritual of the New and the
transposed organs of its declension. (Every
freedom comes with a corpse.) In such
asylum, levied by domination, legions
signify an instinct. Meaning: the enemy is
an exercise in symmetry: us & them. The
answer is to outlast the question and the
symmetry. The code for that is a mind.
And the motion of a mouth is what we
call discourse, the crude claim of a body
infused with surprise (I am, I was, I will

have been). Its one rule is: System needs
its riddle. The fear of chaos is where
power begins, or: Give a Dog a Bone,
leaving behind the power to be, to be
strange, if we're still talking.

●

Through
a Broadband
Swarming

Each Monologue is an aperture onto
excess. Blind, repeatable, in two halves.
A signifying fury exuding its terms. In
its Past, where we operate (mortally), the
Future is anonymous. A 2-person word
that, once uttered, becomes a machine
from having gotten us to think so. It uses
us. We use each other. In corporate units,
inverting the coincidence between the
System and the company that system
keeps. They force us to be the same simple
terms, the domination the workplace frees
us to be: an empty chair indecipherable
from where its abeyance stands. Yet, when
in the course of events, a subset exacts
from us a speech of such imposed mass
that to ingest it inverts that mass, then
we dream, an art between us. The rule

and the exception conveying nothing with
nothing to buy. The pursuit of things and
what follows abandon us in an inversionary
system: Each having that which is in itself
more than itself, forming a sentence, which
begins: "Each having . . . " and so on.
A monetary crisis for which the frontier
is the inverted freedom. (Cf. bag, cf. drag,
cf. black.)

●

The Phantom Limb (it's a head!)

Let they who have not one monster in
their catalectic mind, that screaming pit
at the adjectival extent of things, say to
me: Do something. No one is exempt. Do
something else, I say. Do the first by not
doing the second. Then invert them. See
what happens. For example, the world
turns. Then it stops. We store unrelated
figures in a jar. An impossible crowd. No
organs left. Something is not happening,
and something else is. Nothing is obscure.
For example, people pour up (nel mezzo)
through the organs of their things. Simple
algorithms and simpler things. The world
follows logically: being engenders being.
But the answer is: if the lack of agreement
between code & being hurts nothing or
no one, takes no time and costs nothing,

it isn't a brawl. With no shelf equivalent and no archive, the black bag crawls. Not a pit (Jeremiah, etc.), but the truth of its condition, its condition being inversive non-inclusion in the coordinates of its production. The world is a one-legged brain. This, too, is the history of being dragged.

●

Something's out there, creeping vaguely
in. A or B, even or odd: an impossible
vigilance. Fetishism will be alive when
something's dead. An infernal uniform
worn as the militant index of work. Work
idealizes the world as polarized blind
spots. Old news. We give thanks for these
holes that parataxis may live. A talking
troll's head arising from freedom. Chaos,
of course. The body has no idea it's a
body. Where there's nothing, something's
gained. Anything and nothing. Where
nothing is the inertia of something.

●

2 or 3
leaves
of grass

Poetry is indistinguishable from its existence.
Its form can never be exchanged. It comes.
It goes. Leaving the margin and a barrel for
shooting conventions. A mutual if toothless
alphabet. We can give it away. We can refuse
it and so exercise the power to deny power
its significance. A mirror in the salt pit. In
America and its salty briars & brambles,
citizens are the subjects of a pervasive and so
invisible ritual of the New. It talks to me in
my one new body. Art is only half of it, and
even that half is inverted with nowhere to
point. The road here is the road there. Point
it anywhere and call it parsimony, punching
the zero's into the clown's mouth. The moist
alphabet of Reason.

●

Oedipuscorp @sexless.com

Something is a wall when something (else)
behind it is something (we think) we can't
do without. It creates a kind of specular
braille, a parsimony from inconsistency
between halves of a thus emergent
bicameral brain. Who chooses the wall
chooses incremental reason in the circle
of a concussive logic. Art is nothing until
it opens in Reason. It opens the present to
an incrementally imperfect future when
the past will have evaporated and, in half-
reason (of which it is a part) become a
hole, plugged with a door. A door defines
the state-of-nature: a void to be opened
and then inverted, where inversions
bring a separate art for each inversional
chamber of the brain. The cauldron (or

sack of terms) is patently blind, its one
eye patently shut. Blindly, it parses our
affections parsing the empty wall and
brings the lumpen family in from a
state-of-nature.

●

At this omphalic angle to speech, art is
writing's second life. Its one rule is to say
everything, where everything is the limit
within limits. The future is free of limits.
Something else is there (or was). The absence
of everything that defines us: the fictive
world, the margin, the human condition.
Nothing can fill a condition. Neither art nor
writing nor an empty present. There are
no more monuments to invent, no camel
imagined in its qualitative trek. Irreversible
then, we trek monumentally toward a
condensed, fissional universe in which
the butterflies and the bats are inversions
stencilled on themselves as axioms of what
they signify. Their Being is excision-to-be.
The same and not-the-same.

●

The Quadragene

The Real is an exogamous equation between
common members of the multiple sets it
takes to be. For example, I'm a fly in the
exuberance of romance, counting wings (two
at a time): it affirms me, it affirms me not.
Discipline is one mouth. That mouth exists
for turning repetition into thought while
spreading democracy under a caption that
reads: snip, snip, snip, truth among the brain
rations. Whereas for us, doubt has become a
flashback to saner times in a syntax designed
to blame the noise we make on secrets we
might have learned if only we'd had a syntax.
Meaning: take the money. Put it in the wall
and skip the romance, where our one feature
is mobile and strong: Being in the double
negative present.

●

The monogene called Me!

The dream of an existence is its
extremity, either a scissive sea or, at
its limit, the senses reproduced sans
awe. I, the dreamer, circle the wagons
(the flies, bats, and nameless rats) from
the wallpaper of my existence. Into
the mirror we go. Where I see myself
dissolving into itself at the far end of an
inverse hole, a delirium in indigestible
flux. I am nothing if not a wall between
flux and delirium, a blindfold asking of
fixed reason one eye or another to be
the runway in my alphabet, which is
the truth of the impossible: we want,
therefore, we invert (dissolve) into
the spectral head putting terms in the
terms that put them there. An unbent

dominance in the periplum's double back, or eyeful (in halves). Where every bullet has a solipsist behind it. I can't remember my wager.

●

Capt. America has been shot!

This is a fricative life. If by fricative we
don't mean free. At its limits, anything
is free, the arithmetic in which those
are drawers that were Padgett's eyes.
Nothing(1) in that one and nothing(2) in
me. Inscrutable power has no content
other than what language fulfills in the
present. For example, take one perishable
figure and one cartoon frame. The
figure floats in its own speech bubble,
in the frame. Speech bubbles are the
ultimate conspiracy machines, within
which we (as the State) exist as states
of naïveté, useful to litigants and the
uninverted: Blob v. Blob. But where
property (intellectual or otherwise) is the
corpse of a corpse, a hole in the empty

set of Reason. Even the reverse is true. A
unity brought on by prison. What we are
and what I am fall somewhere between
the bars and the ocean. In our blind,
insurmountable syntax, we can't tell one
from none. I am this. We are nouns (in the
specular state).

●

Let's leave it here (and that, there). The
alarm (in us) where sum and sun climb.
There's no business like no business. The
semantics of it don't matter. Business is
binary. Any desert is the perfect road. The
shortest route between non-existent points
in the periploi of inversions. The disaster
of capital is that it begins with an end, a
milestone (or rule) in a distance impossible
to cross except by halves and inversions.
We come to any whole as an accord
that that thing imposes, an institutional
inversion. The desert didn't exist. We
didn't cross it. End of the First Half.

●

Prosperocidal

Molly & Peter say: Write a letter. Fold it
one time, top to bottom, and place it in the
top right pocket. Remove the letter already
there, fold it once, left to right, and place
it in the top left pocket, at the same time
removing the letter there, folding right to
left, moving it to the left of center middle
pocket, shifting and folding the letter
there to the right of center middle, right
of center middle to bottom left, bottom
left to bottom right. Discard the bottom
right letter in a method to be devised. And
repeat.

●

People happen. They don't exist. The
monsters get rich and then get rich. A magic
bullet in an elevator of inexplicable dread,
running on the tiled specter of flesh. In one
hole and then another, familiar and weird,
wondering what happened. What happens
is a symptom that makes us think that
something happens. In which you put your
money down and play, hoping for something
amid all the spectral stars & stripes. Where
my eyes, a version of the mole hole, have
fingers (still translucent and protruding) to
drive them with. Even a little mystery robs
meaning of its comeback. I push, and it
rolls. Other than that, who can say what it
sounds like, looks like, is, the monotone rose
of the world?

●

Walking a human who's 50 in megalomaniac years

No matter how violent the simulacra
become, nothing will undo what we have
done. To be right, you have to change
into a bystander and be impossible to
find. A voiceprint without a voice, its
contradictions fading into grammar.
Hysteria can't be far behind, and its
demand for complete freedom – part
parsimony, part compensation for
everything else. Not this. Just a promise
that art has to be work. And if it comes to
more, More is more. Its surplus an X by
means of which something is something
else. Not that it was anything but "not
that" in the transferential era since not
being anything else. Where we put our
symptoms in a bag and call it free. In the
altercidal fallacies of our self-inflected sea.

•

The one oath of poetry we believe in is
that art exceeds its target. Its target might
be outrage, or it might be hysteria. In
its custodial subset, my Bedlam is the
Brain, a frame to be lively in, the minute
particulars of which are the margins
othering the night away. The System
never sleeps and so doesn't dream.
Without imagination, it doesn't exist.
The fly's wing isn't anxious. It thinks
in an alphabet of mutual freedom: Read
my terms and I'll read yours. The thetic
standard is that language is a transaction
between "no one" and "someone." The
antic horizon to a simple neuronal task
(one of a dozen, no more). I.e., there is no
magic term which, having left its thetic

cartridge, wanders through our flesh,
signifying everything. I'll read your terms.
You read mine.

●

May my lack be nimble
and the codes be quick,
as the neurons assemble
in the Big Board's trick.

●

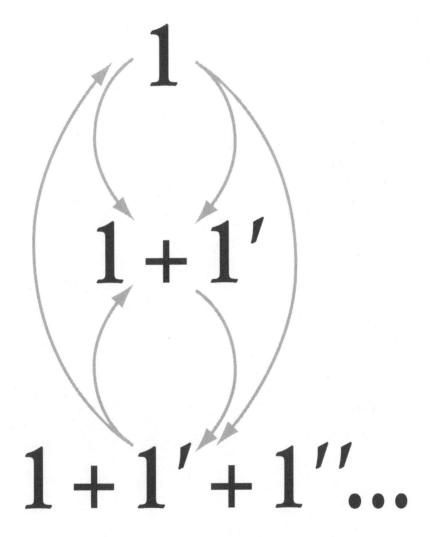

As the client of a nation having woven
violence & self-loathing so starkly within its
ruinous operation that to be myself I must
hide myself, let me state here and always
that this useless, national strategy
of embracing contradiction (even of nothing,
to the POINT of nothing) is not a figure in
anyone's imagined future but is and will
be here and everywhere if so pursued the
absence of all existence because it is only
in the facts of our proximal extensions, an
imaginal life, that our existence comes to
be at all. I do NOT bind myself to death.
I will NOT limit my work in order to
eternalize it (end quote) nor will I offer even
one penny of my human capital to national
renewal unless it is irrevocably in the
interests of a ONE. THIS is MY ars poetica.

●

Larry Price emerged (records indicate) in a small farming village in Northern California. But such records (from the heart of gold rush country) are notoriously unreliable. A fiction, at best. Thus, school in Santa Barbara, school in San Francisco and, at long last, the dawn of reason. Next, relocation to New Jersey where elusiveness is an indispensable tactic. Previous books include *Crude Thinking* and *Circadium*.

The Quadragene inverts set theory only to find both nothing *and* something in those drawers that, 40 years ago, a New York poet first documented as empty. These frames with referents—hardly still lifes—reverse a specular pair ("both are neither"), allowing it to be ground for future lenses without distorting the contemporary realism of our blobs. Here the word "bag" is commutative with Duncan's "life-shape" and systemic arrows circle overhead—a demonstration of practical doubt our author has the strength of mind to accept.

—*Miles Champion*

Between shadow and ground, imagination populates from memory: no things but in nothings. I enjoy *Quadragene* for its echoes and its range; for its driving me occasionally to the dictionary from interest rather than as obligation; for its elegant and intelligent design... and for causing me to think about fat and epilepsy and the view from at sea. Self-explanatory, it is a Mother Gooseflesh for now.

—*Tom Raworth*

Larry Price's ars poetica follows the money to the ends of art, where on a good day "what we mean to say buries us in our own terms." That is, the bristling prose poems of *The Quadragene* propel us ("vexed humans") to the "antic horizon" of meaning by way of spectacularly irreducible and wholly entertaining argument.

—*Jean Day*

ROOF BOOKS

THE BEST IN LANGUAGE SINCE 1976

- ANDREWS, BRUCE. CO. COLLABORATIONS WITH BARBARA COLE, JESSE FREEMAN, JESSICA GRIM, YEDDA MORRISON, KIM ROSEFIELD. 104P. $12.95.
- ANDREWS, BRUCE. EX WHY ZEE. 112P. $10.95.
- ANDREWS, BRUCE. GETTING READY TO HAVE BEEN FRIGHTENED. 116P. $7.50, OP.
- ARAKAWA & GINS, MADELINE. MAKING DYING ILLEGAL. 224P. $22.95.
- BENSON, STEVE. BLUE BOOK. COPUB. WITH THE FIGURES. 250P. $12.50
- BERNSTEIN, CHARLES. CONTROLLING INTERESTS. 80P. $11.95.
- BERNSTEIN, CHARLES. ISLETS/IRRITATIONS. 112P. $9.95.
- BERNSTEIN, CHARLES (EDITOR). THE POLITICS OF POETIC FORM. 246P. $12.95; CLOTH $21.95.
- BROSSARD, NICOLE. PICTURE THEORY. 188P. $11.95.
- CADIOT, OLIVIER. FORMER, FUTURE, FUGITIVE. TRANSLATED BY COLE SWENSEN. 166P. $13.95.
- CHAMPION, MILES. THREE BELL ZERO. 72P. $10.95.
- CHILD, ABIGAIL. FROM SOLIDS. 36P. LIMITED EDITION. $20.
- CHILD, ABIGAIL. SCATTER MATRIX. 79P. $9.95.
- DAVIES, ALAN. ACTIVE 24 HOURS. 100P. $5.
- DAVIES, ALAN. SIGNAGE. 184P. $11.
- DAVIES, ALAN. RAVE. 64P. $7.95.
- DAY, JEAN. A YOUNG RECRUIT. 58P. $6.
- DI PALMA, RAY. MOTION OF THE CYPHER. 112P. $10.95.
- DI PALMA, RAY. RAIK. 100P. $9.95.
- DORIS, STACY. KILDARE. 104P. $9.95.
- DORIS, STACY. CHEERLEADER'S GUIDE TO THE WORLD: COUNCIL BOOK 88P. $12.95.
- DREYER, LYNNE. THE WHITE MUSEUM. 80P. $12.
- DWORKIN, CRAIG. STRAND. 112P. $12.95.
- DWORKIN, CRAIG, EDITOR. THE CONSEQUENCE OF INNOVATION: 21ST CENTURY POETICS. 304P. $29.95
- EDWARDS, KEN. GOOD SCIENCE. 80P. $9.95.
- EIGNER, LARRY. AREAS LIGHTS HEIGHTS. 182P. $12, $22 (CLOTH).
- GARDNER, DREW. PETROLEUM HAT. 96P. $12.95.
- GIZZI, MICHAEL. CONTINENTAL HARMONIES. 96P. $8.95.
- GLADMAN, RENEE. A PICTURE-FEELING. 72P. $10.95.
- GOLDMAN, JUDITH. VOCODER. 96P. $11.95.
- GORDON, NADA. FOLLY. 128P. $13.95
- GOTTLIEB, MICHAEL. NINETY-SIX TEARS. 88P. $5.
- GOTTLIEB, MICHAEL. GORGEOUS PLUNGE. 96P. $11.95.
- GOTTLIEB, MICHAEL. LOST & FOUND. 80P. $11.95.
- GREENWALD, TED. JUMPING THE LINE. 120P. $12.95.
- GRENIER, ROBERT. A DAY AT THE BEACH. 80P. $6.
- GROSMAN, ERNESTO. THE XULREADER: AN ANTHOLOGY OF ARGENTINE POETRY (1981–1996). 167P. $14.95.
- GUEST, BARBARA. DÜRER IN THE WINDOW, REFLEXIONS ON ART. BOOK DESIGN BY RICHARD TUTTLE. FOUR COLOR THROUGHOUT. 80P. $24.95.
- HILLS, HENRY. MAKING MONEY. 72P. $7.50. VHS VIDEOTAPE $24.95. BOOK & TAPE $29.95.
- HUANG YUNTE. SHI: A RADICAL READING OF CHINESE POETRY. 76P. $9.95
- HUNT, ERICA. LOCAL HISTORY. 80 P. $9.95.
- KUSZAI, JOEL (EDITOR) POETICS@, 192 P. $13.95.
- INMAN, P. CRISS CROSS. 64 P. $7.95.
- INMAN, P. RED SHIFT. 64P. $6.
- LAZER, HANK. DOUBLESPACE. 192 P. $12.
- LEVY, ANDREW. PAPER HEAD LAST LYRICS. 112 P. $11.95.

- MAC LOW, JACKSON. REPRESENTATIVE WORKS: 1938–1985. 360P. $18.95 (CLOTH).
- MAC LOW, JACKSON. TWENTIES. 112P. $8.95.
- MCMORRIS, MARK. THE CAFÉ AT LIGHT. 112P. $12.95.
- MORIARTY, LAURA. RONDEAUX. 107P. $8.
- NASDOR, MARC. SONNETAILIA. 80P. $12.95
- NEILSON, MELANIE. CIVIL NOIR. 96P. $8.95.
- OSMAN, JENA. AN ESSAY IN ASTERISKS. 112P. $12.95.
- PEARSON, TED. PLANETARY GEAR. 72P. $8.95.
- PERELMAN, BOB. VIRTUAL REALITY. 80P. $9.95.
- PERELMAN, BOB. THE FUTURE OF MEMORY. 120P. $14.95.
- PERELMAN, BOB. IFLIFE. 140P. $13.95.
- PIOMBINO, NICK, THE BOUNDARY OF BLUR. 128P. $13.95.
- PRIZE BUDGET FOR BOYS, THE SPECTACULAR VERNACULAR REVUE. 96P. $14.95.
- RAWORTH, TOM. CLEAN & WELL-LIT. 106P. $10.95.
- ROBINSON, KIT. BALANCE SHEET. 112P. $11.95.
- ROBINSON, KIT. DEMOCRACY BOULEVARD. 104P. $9.95.
- ROBINSON, KIT. ICE CUBES. 96P. $6.
- ROSENFIELD, KIM. GOOD MORNING—MIDNIGHT—. 112P. $10.95.
- SCALAPINO, LESLIE. OBJECTS IN THE TERRIFYING TENSE LONGING FROM TAKING PLACE. 88P. $9.95.
- SEATON, PETER. THE SON MASTER. 64P. $5.
- SHAW, LYTLE, EDITOR. NINETEEN LINES: A DRAWING CENTER WRITING ANTHOLOGY. 336P. $24.95
- SHERRY, JAMES. POPULAR FICTION. 84P. $6.
- SILLIMAN, RON. THE NEW SENTENCE. 200P. $10.
- SILLIMAN, RON. N/O. 112P. $10.95.
- SMITH, ROD. MUSIC OR HONESTY. 96P. $12.95
- SMITH, ROD. PROTECTIVE IMMEDIACY. 96P. $9.95
- STEFANS, BRIAN KIM. FREE SPACE COMIX. 96P. $9.95
- STEFANS, BRIAN KIM. KLUGE. 128P. $13.95
- SULLIVAN, GARY. PPL IN A DEPOT. 104P. $13.95.
- TARKOS, CHRISTOPHE. MA LANGUE EST POÉTIQUE—SELECTED WORKS. 96P. $12.95.
- TEMPLETON, FIONA. CELLS OF RELEASE. 128P. WITH PHOTOGRAPHS. $13.95.
- TEMPLETON, FIONA. YOU—THE CITY. 150P. $11.95.
- TORRES, EDWIN. THE ALL-UNION DAY OF THE SHOCK WORKER. 112 P. $10.95.
- TYSH, CHRIS. CLEAVAGE. 96P. $11.95.
- WARD, DIANE. HUMAN CEILING. 80P. $8.95.
- WARD, DIANE. RELATION. 64P. $7.50.
- WATSON, CRAIG. FREE WILL. 80P. $9.95.
- WATTEN, BARRETT. PROGRESS. 122P. $7.50.
- WEINER, HANNAH. WE SPEAK SILENT. 76 P. $9.95
- WEINER, HANNAH. PAGE. 136 P. $12.95
- WELLMAN, MAC. MINIATURE. 112 P. $12.95
- WELLMAN, MAC. STRANGE ELEGIES. 96 P. $12.95
- WOLSAK, LISSA. PEN CHANTS. 80P. $9.95.
- YASUSADA, ARAKI. DOUBLED FLOWERING: FROM THE NOTEBOOKS OF ARAKI YASUSADA. 272P. $14.95.

ROOF BOOKS ARE PUBLISHED BY
SEGUE FOUNDATION • 300 BOWERY • NEW YORK, NY 10012
VISIT OUR WEBSITE AT SEGUEFOUNDATION.COM

ROOF BOOKS ARE DISTRIBUTED BY
SMALL PRESS DISTRIBUTION
1341 SEVENTH STREET • BERKELEY, CA. 94710-1403.
PHONE ORDERS: 800-869-7553
SPDBOOKS.ORG